Desert Images

of SAUDI ARABIA

Desert Images

of SAUDI ARABIA

Garth Hyland

Endpapers:
Course grains of sand from the desert plains west of Tabuk. Magnification is approximately six times.

Opposite title page:
A spotted eagle owl (Bubo africanus) photographed in a rocky outcrop north of Dukhneh in the Qassim region.

Title Page:
Close-up of beetle tracks in the Ad Dahna dunes east of Riyadh.

Below:
Dunes at Thumamah.

Opposite page:
A plain tiger butterfly (Danus chrysippus) at Rawdhat Kareem.

Published by Garth Hyland
C/- P.O. Box 622, Riyadh 11421
Kingdom of Saudi Arabia

First Edition 1997

All photos, design, text and page layouts by Garth Hyland.

Printed in Hong Kong by the South China Printing Company (1988) Limited.

Colour Reproduction by Universal Colour Scanning Ltd.

King Fahd National Library Cataloging-in-Publication Data
Hyland, Garth
   Desert Images of Saudi Arabia - Riyadh
   180p, 30cm
   ISBN: 9960-31-621-1
1-Saudi Arabia - Description and travel   2. - Geography - Saudi Arabia   1 - Title
   915.31 dc   1530/17

Legal Deposit No. 1530/17
ISBN: 9960-31-621-1

Author's Introduction

This book is not meant to be an exhaustive record of places, flora or fauna in the Kingdom of Saudi Arabia. It is a record of things that have interested me from a photographic and inquisitive environmental perspective in the areas where I have been fortunate to spend some time. Undoubtedly, there are other equally interesting areas of the Kingdom which I have not visited and their omission is only due to lack of material rather than a bias towards certain areas.

The areas covered by geographic chapter titles are fairly loose and include areas bordering onto the main areas described. In some cases, however, I have stretched the boundaries a little in order to allow me to include some things which greatly interested me.

The adventure of preparing for this book has been a great journey of experiences and discovery about the Kingdom and its many hidden treasures. No doubt the bedu know their environment intimately but it is a thrill for an outsider to be able to see, for the first time, and photograph the spectacular and often beautiful scenery as well as the flora and all creatures, great and small, which dwell in this Kingdom.

Garth Hyland

Dunes near Dilim.

CONTENTS

CHAPTER ONE

INTRODUCTION

Desert areas and centres covered in this book.

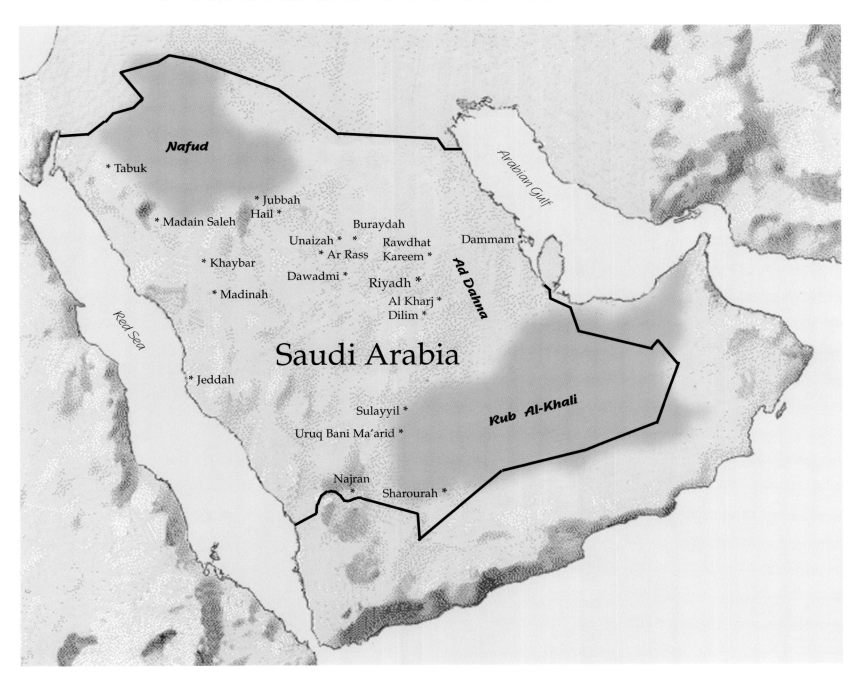

Saudi Arabia conjures up a picture of great expanses of sand dunes but, while there is no shortage of them, there are only two major areas of sandy desert in the Kingdom. They are the Rub al-Khali (known as the Empty Quarter) in the south-east and the Great Nafud Desert in the north-west.

The Rub al-Khali is approximately 640,000 square kilometres in area making it one of the largest continuous stretches of sand in the world. It is a forbidding place where temperatures regularly soar into the 50 degree celcius range during the summer months.

The area, as its name implies, is largely unpopulated and crossings are reserved for the most intrepid adventurers or, more recently, those who are fortunate enough to possess vehicles such as the "Hummer" which can tackle the great waste with confidence. I have been told by those who have travelled there, however, that even in the most remote regions of the desert it is not unusual to see a pickup truck appear over the top of a sand dune, itself a testimony to the incredible skills of the bedu in the hostile environment in which they live.

The Rub al-Khali is actually linked to the Great Nafud Desert by a narrow band about 50 kilometres in width and which arcs towards the east coast before turning back towards the Nafud. This extension is called the Ad Dahna sand belt and provides one of the prettiest sights between Riyadh and Dammam.

The band joining the two major deserts has fingers which extend for several kilometres along the way. For example, between Riyadh and Buraydah, two such

These sand mountains of the Rub al-Khali (Empty Quarter) continue unbroken for over 1000 kilometres from east of Najran to Eastern UAE.

fingers are encountered just past Al-Ghat.

The Great Nafud desert is less than a tenth the size of the Rub al-Khali but nevertheless has some massive dunes as high as 90 metres. The sand of the Nafud is generally red like the sands of the Ad Dahna, both being stained by iron oxide.

Like parts of the Rub al-Khali, the Nafud has many longitudinal sand dunes known as uruq. Satellite maps show that these often extend for many kilometres. In the excellent publication, "Deserts -

The Encroaching Wilderness" a desert is defined in terms of its ability to support life and describes the Kingdom of Saudi Arabia as mainly desert with most of the remainder as semi arid. There are vast expanses of gravel plains in the Kingdom which are effectively deserts in the sense that they support little life and in the hot summer months are as deadly as their sandy counterparts in their threat to life. Another geological feature of the Kingdom which in many cases could be classified as desert consists of mudstone and limestone "moun-

The effect of clouds on this landscape near Unaizah in the Qassim region creates a wonderfully soft picture of a weekend camp.

Gravel hills past Dilim leading towards the Rub al-Khali. At certain times of the day in winter and spring the colours in the hills can be quite beautiful whereas in the full heat of a summer day the impression is one of barren, drab danger.

tains", escarpments and barren plains which are remnants, in many instances, of an ancient era when the Arabian Peninsula was submerged. In many cases evidence of volcanic activity is also littered over both mountains and plains. It is not uncommon to find areas with fossilised shells and coral, sometimes in perfect condition. It is amazing, considering that the peninsula was submerged many millions of years ago, that one can still walk across the plains and escarpments and find such fossils.

Over time the escarpments have eroded, in the process producing impressive cliffs dropping up to several hundred metres to the sloping spoil and plains below. Other mountains, for example those beyond Dilim and approaching the Rub al-Khali, are more like rolling hills of gravel with no escarpments at all.

In the above photo the hills rollover into large sand dunes and on into the Rub al-Khali. Little vegetation grows on the hills themselves although, in the valleys, eroded material and water combine to support substantial populations of camels, sheep, goats and other life.

Opposite:
This interesting mix of mudstone and gravel hills together with plains littered with black volcanic rock is near Al Kharj.

Modern technology has combined with a great determination to produce from a land which, on the surface, appears so barren that nothing would seem to be capable of being produced. The regions of Qassim and Al Kharj produce great amounts of feedstock and wheat from circular farms which, in many cases, bound directly onto sandy desert. When flying over the Qassim region one can see hundreds of circular farms side by side stretching towards the horizon. When viewed from the ground on a hot and dusty day it seems even more incredible that man has managed to conquer the environment to such an extent.

The contrast between rich green feedstock, red sand, distant light purple escarpment and azure blue sky provides one of the memorable landscapes in the Najd region and another example of the diversity of desert images in the Kingdom.

Photography is very dependent on the available light and light intensity and there is plenty of both in the Kingdom. I prefer to take most photos in the early morning since the light is very soft and landscapes are extremely beautiful. In addition, the early morning just after dawn is the most likely time to see animals such as foxes before it either

This farm near Dilim south-west of Al Kharj vividly illustrates the proximity of the desert. The irrigation water, distributed by computer controlled booms, comes from drill holes which are being sunk to ever increasing depths due to the heavy demands of farmers.

becomes too hot or other interlopers, such as man, arrive on the scene. Early morning is also the time when one can savour the pleasant coolness of the winter or the bearable warmth of the summer before the heat begins to intensify. The silence of the early morning in the desert and the anticipation of finding some new animal life makes it a very pleasurable time. It is the time when fresh tracks of the night before can lead to a gerbils hole or a foxes lair. It is the time when the seemingly frenzied activity of lizards, mice, gerbils, jerboas and beetles leave their criss-crossed tracks freshly in the sand.

A major feature around the Riyadh area is the number of escarpments which drop away suddenly several hundred metres to the plains below. The best known is the Tuwayq escarpment which runs from just south of Buraydah some 300 kilometres north-west of Riyadh to south of Wadi Ad Dawasir, southwest of Riyadh, a total of some 800 kilometres. It represents a lasting memory west of Riyadh where the main road to Makkah and Jeddah descends through a spectacular cutting to the plain below. There are many other escarpments around Riyadh with numerous wadis in between.

This landscape near Al Kharj is typical of the gravel and sand plains adjacent to escarpments in the Najd region. "Citrullus colocynthis" (foreground) is a fleshy gourd which is common in summer months.

Opposite:
The Tuwayq Escarpment west of Riyadh. This is a common sight for all travellers on the Riyadh - Jeddah road. The old road to Makkah and Jeddah actually runs parallel to this escarpment for some distance on the way to Durma.

Opposite:
The deserted mud houses appear as though they are about to be swallowed up by the massive sand dunes on the edge of the Great Nafud Desert not far from Hail.

Nowhere is the fragility of the co-existence between human habitation an the desert more clearly demonstrated than on the fringes of the Nafud Desert around Hail. There is evidence of villages which have been abandoned because of the encroaching sands and others where the battle is still being fought. In the end, however, the desert will be the victor. The sheer quantity of sand built up in the mighty dunes which sweep down from the Nafud appears to be irresistible.

There are those, however, who choose to live in the desert rather than on the edge of it. The bedu live in the manner they have been used to for centuries but with the added comfort of water tankers rather then sunk wells and the benefit of satellite dishes. In all other respects their life is in concert with the elements with all the accompanying hardships .

The constant shifting of camp, as pastures run out and the distance to drive sheep, goats and camels each day becomes too long, adds another necessary burden on the desert dwellers.

Despite their hardships, the bedu are among the most hospitable people one will find anywhere.

This bedu camp on the very edge of the Nafud is blessed with much vegetation following exceptional winter and spring rains.

19

The desert blooms after winter and spring rains. Often unpredictable, the rains can produce much damage, as the run-off occurs, but also much needed vegetation for animals of all sizes.

The dunes take on an entirely different character in the winter and early spring. After rains the dunes become a motley colour where water has either washed down particles of darker material or has simply not dried out. In addition, the lack of wind results in dunes without sharp ridges and presents a softer but generally less attractive picture.

In the cooler winter months much of the animal life "goes to sleep" literally and it is difficult to find life with the same ease as in the spring. Following the rains the desert blooms and a great burst of energy is generated. The whole life cycle of the ecosystem is regulated to a large extent by the degree of rain during a season. For example in 1996 the rains were the best for many years. One of the results was grasshoppers in many areas in almost plague proportions. They extended into the main streets of Riyadh where it was difficult to walk without treading on them. The flowers of the desert also burst forth in great numbers,

The Ad Dahna dunes situated about 100 kilometres east of Riyadh en route to Dammam. The effect of recent spring rains is evident on the large sand mountain in the rear of the photo. Notice the soft roundness of the dunes which is typical of winter and early spring.

Floodwaters flowing across a desert plain near Dawadmi, west of Riyadh. The rains had been heavy and the run-off fast and full.

in some cases painting the landscape with a coloured hue for kilometres across the gravel plains.

The wildlife of the desert must fluctuate with the fortunes of the seasons. Good rains will produce more offspring which the food chain will support until the time when the rains fail and the food chain falters. Life needs food and water and there is no second chance when they fail. Nature regulates itself here as elsewhere with predictable effects on wildlife. The uncertainty of the seasons in the desert places a tremendous strain on the ecosystem. Fortunately there is not the same threat to wildlife environ-

ments in the Kingdom as in other countries where forests are being cut down at an alarming rate. Hunting can still take its toll and animals such as the Arabian Oryx were almost extinguished before being reintroduced through a far-sighted program controlled by the National Commission for Wildlife Conservation and Development (NCWCD). This body has greatly contributed to the growth in numbers of many indigenous species and has expanded the reserves it operates in a manner which will allow coexistence with native bedu but preserving, at the same time, the wonderfully rich wildlife heritage of the Kingdom.

One of my biggest surprises was to learn that Arabian Oryx actually survive in the Rub al-Khali. At the wildlife reserve of Uruq Bani Ma'arid the NCWCD has released a quantity of Arabian Oryx as well as many gazelle from the breeding stations at Taif and Thumamah. These herds are thriving on the unex-pected amount of vegetation which grows on the plains between the rows of sand mountains known as uruq. The reserve is carefully controlled and parts are set aside for traditional hunting while in other parts it is strictly forbid-den. It is an interesting experiment which has all the hallmarks of success.

The extent of wildlife in Saudi Arabia is captured in the 1982 publication "Animal Life in Saudi Arabia" by Betty A Lipscombe Vincett. It is difficult to see , in the wild, many of the animals shown in that publication but the more time one spends in the desert the more one sees. One interesting "oasis", which has sprung up since the blossoming of Riyadh as a large city, is the river at Al Hair which is actually the treated efflu-ent from the city sewerage. The area surrounding this river is covered with trees, reeds and shrubs which have become the home of numerous species of birdlife which have either become permanent residents or temporary ones on their migration paths between Europe/Russia and Africa. The two birds above would be more at home in the water but were found on a road sign in the middle of 250 kilometres of sand

These Cattle Egrets (Bubulcus ibis) were totally out of place in the middle of a 250 Km stretch of road leading to Sharourah through the Rub al-Khali. They could only sur-vive on the water of nearby bedu camps.

dunes in the Rub al-Khali - obviously lost but apparently surviving, probably on the water of nearby bedu camps.

Insect life is perhaps more plentiful than larger species and in springtime, triggered by new flowers, a whole host of insects and butterflies emerge for their brief sojourn in the delicate desert environment. They are part of an often unique web of life that adds much needed colour to a harsh land. They greatly enhanced the photographic opportunities for my "desert images" of Saudi Arabia.

Opposite:
This blanket of flowers following good spring rains near Buraydah extended as far as the eye could see.

A colourful beetle feeding on the nectar of an acacia tree on a desert plain north of Durma.

CHAPTER TWO

NAJD

Previous page:
Late afternoon sun on the Tuwayq Escarpment west of Riyadh.

Among my favourite places in the vicinity of Riyadh are the sand dunes of Ad Dahna about 100 kilometres towards Dammam. The area is near where the old Dammam road is joined to the new Dammam road by an extension which encloses a strip of wonderful dunes with a huge sand mountain at its centre. The strip varies from a few hundred metres to several kilometres and is home to many of the smaller animals, such as gerbils and gerboa as well as a shifting population of beautiful sand foxes.

The area is not bordered by a centre of population and is frequented only by weekenders who tend not to venture too far into the dunes. This provides an environment which is relatively safe for the animals which live there and is one of generally pristine beauty.

The sand is mostly coloured with iron oxide and takes on a reddish appearance at times in the early morning and late afternoon. Some dunes, however, exhibit colours more generally called "sandy". After rains the whole complex of dunes

Early spring after plentiful rains saw two new additions to this family of foxes in Ad Dahna.

becomes a mix of light and dark as sand grains of different sizes and weights are washed down the slopes to differing degrees and the moisture from the rain remains near the surface. The sand pat- terns at different times of the year pre- sent, in the early morning, many won- derful photographic opportunities. The following pages reflect some of the images I have collected from Ad Dahna.

Beetle tracks on a dune at Ad Dahna.

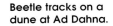

Page 30:
Ad Dahna dunes

Page 31:
An Arabian toad-headed agama lizard on the Ad Dahna dunes.

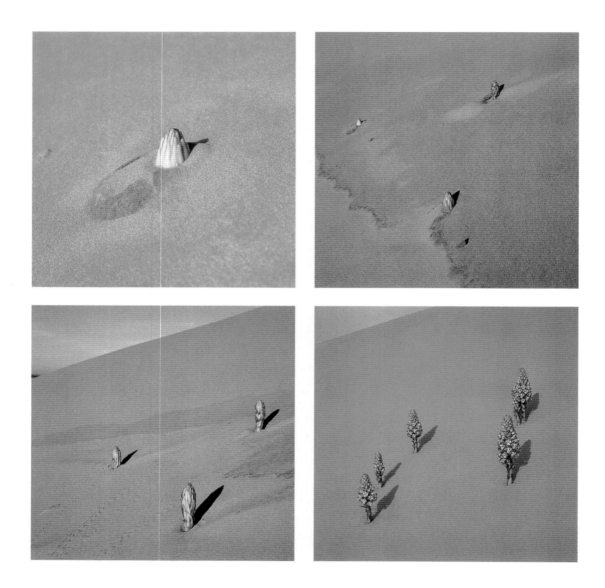

This cluster of "Cistanche tubulosa" (desert hyacinth) was first seen emerging from the sand near the top of a large dune in Ad Dahna. The top left photo was taken on 18.1.'96, top right on 25.1.'96, bottom left on 1.2.'96 and bottom right on 16.2.'96. The plant can grow to a height of 40 centimetres or so and adds some extra beauty to the desert landscape. The small flowers are about 1 to 2 cm. in diameter. It is widespread throughout the Kingdom. The photo on page 33 shows a close-up of the flowers of the Cistanche tubulosa.

Left:
Flowers of "Cistanche tubulosa" (desert hyacinth).

Overleaf:

Page 34:
Dunes near Dilim.

Page 35:
A gerbil busy foraging in the Ad Dahna dunes.

The main road from Riyadh to Jeddah veers to the southwest and descends the escarpment through a gigantic cutting before entering onto a gravel plain several kilometres wide. At the other side of the plain the road branches with one arm being the old road to Makkah and Jeddah. This road heads northwest and passes through some very attractive country on its way to towns such as Durma, Marat and Shaqra.

The terrain is largely gravel plains although one encounters some dunes near Shaqra. Escarpments serve as impressive backdrops for a large part of the journey.

During early autumn and spring the journey can be quite spectacular with fresh winds scudding clouds across the sky, casting hundreds of shadows across the landscape and creating some very different effects for the photographer.

Most of the following photos were taken during one such memorable trip.

Opposite:
A solitary tent is dwarfed by the escarpment on the way to Durma, west of Riyadh.

Below:
Ruins near Ar Raghabah northwest of Riyadh.

A young camel trailing behind the herd with the Tuwayq Escarpment as a backdrop.

<u>Opposite:</u>
The contrast of blue sky, ashen escarpment, red sand and bright green feedstock near Shaqra.

A flat topped
mountain near Ar
Raghabah with
an unusual early
morning cloud.

Opposite:
Bright sunlight breaks
through a cloudy autumn
sky to create a highlight
of the shepherd and his
flock near Durma.

Floodwaters lap-
ping the road to
Durma after the
heaviest rains in
decades.

Opposite:
Farm in the lee of
red sand dunes
near Shaqra.

Left:
A Little Green Bee-eater waits for its insect or butterfly meal to come within range in the Durma area.

Opposite:
Spotted eagle owls photographed north of Dukhneh in the Qassim region.

Below:
A lacertid (Acanthodactylus schmidti) lizard sunning itself out-side its hole in the Qassim region.

I was interested to explore the Qassim area and a colleague directed me to the Ar Rass area. The area just north of Dukhneh consists of sandy desert plains littered with small and large hills of granite which has weathered over time. The region proved to be very fruitful and we located a group of eight or so owls which were obviously doing well on the large numbers of smaller animal life on which the owls would prey. I have included two photos here since I particularly liked the way they allowed us to approach openly within 600mm distance. You will need to look carefully at the photo below to spot four owls rather than three. While we were watching they went through all sorts of stretching exercises with their wings and necks. Their camouflage was almost perfect.

Overleaf:
Page 47: One of the family of spotted eagle owls north of Dukhneh and its meal? on page 46.

Granite hills rising
from the sandy
desert plains
north of Dukhneh
in the Qassim
region.

These thistles, Echinops spinosa were photographed north of Dukhneh, Qassim region.

Granite hills in the process of decomposition at the hands of the elements - north of Dukhneh, Qassim region.

A shepherd battling his way through a raging sandstorm north of Majma'ah with his flock. We had travelled through 250 kilometres of the storm when we encountered him off to the side of the road.

This agama lizard in the Qassim region matched in with its surroundings perfectly.

This green field was photographed near Al Ghada Parks not far from Unaizah in the Qassim region. Note the ever-present dunes in the background.

Taken just after heavy rains this normally dry plain became a temporary lake with a beautiful effect. The water is only centimetres deep and lasts only a few weeks or less before it dries up completely.

These three photos were taken near Al Ghat, just before Buraydah and Unaizeh in the Qassim region. The vast lake in the top photo covered several square kilometres for a short time. A visit a few weeks later revealed extensive salt flats without water.

The middle photo shows a tranquil farm nestled in between the sand dunes and a small escarpment. The sheep are grazing on the stubble remaining after harvesting crops from a circular irrigated field.

The bottom photo shows circular irrigated fields right in the midst of the sand dunes. It seems incongruous that next to hot desert sand one can have flourishing green fields of feedstock or wheat.

<u>Opposite:</u>
This strange mix of stone mountain and sand dunes was taken near Dawadmi west of Riyadh.

Rawdhat Kareem is a pretty area of permanent green near the town of Gilana on the road to Rumah, to the northeast of Riyadh. Many of the surrounding wadis run off into this area and the floodwaters feed a considerable area of growth which provides a very attractive picnic area. The area abounds with birdlife and insects and after a good rain in spring it bursts into a blaze of colour for some weeks. The reserve ends fairly abruptly on one side where it butts into a long length of sand dunes which adds to the overall attractiveness of the site.

What appears from above to be grass turns out to be more like a tree stump with grass as its foliage. Nature, through this Calligonum comosum, has evolved a cunning way of preventing the "grass" from being washed away when a heavy run-off occurs.

Spring comes to Rawdhat Kareem. For the next few months the area will become a picture of colour and a haven for insects, butterflies and birds.

Opposite:
This "temporary" river at Gilana comes to life whenever there is a good rain . It drains into Rawdhat Kareem with other run-offs to create a permanent reserve of green in the midst of the desert. As the water sub-sides along the river the mud dries into very interesting pat-terns, colours and shapes.

The "Painted Lady" butterfly - Vanessa cardui, is from the Nymphalidae family and is very common around Riyadh and other parts of the Kingdom. It is seen here on ground which has dried and cracked after good spring rains.

"Poekilcerus bufonius vittatus" are quite prolific in the desert areas. This mating pair was taken at Rawdhat Kareem northeast of Riyadh.

Al Kharj and the surrounding region is a significant wheat and crop growing area. The countryside is so green along a strip following the main road that one could be forgiven for thinking that one was in parts of Europe. There are many trees, shrubs and green fields but only a short distance away are the ever present sand dunes or plains. Near Dilim, further west from Al Kharj, one can see the dunes ranging down towards the Rub al-Khali. An early morning trip through the region can be very rewarding especially when the sun rises over the green fields and the sand to show a unique land-scape to say the least.

Sunrise over an irrigated field at Al Kharj south of Riyadh.

This field of irrigated feed crops is one of many located adjacent to sand dunes near Dilim, west of Al Kharj.

Sand dunes on a beautiful day near Dilim.

Right:
A small Senna Italica making a start in the dunes at Dilim.

These pigeon "lofts" were on a small property adjoining the road to Haradh, east of Al Kharj. The property was bounded on the other side by a sandy desert plain. A small quantity of goats was also kept under the shelter.

The old railway, which joined Riyadh and Dammam, runs through the desert and is seen here in the vicinity of a small town some distance past Al Kharj.

An area closer to Riyadh which is picturesque and a playground for Saudis and expatriates alike is beyond the Tuwayq Escarpment and on towards Hafirat Nisah. The area commonly known as the "Red Sand Dunes" creates some wonderful landscapes, especially late in the afternoons. Some sunsets are spectacular and combine with the red dunes to provide memorable moments of solitude.

A common sport there is driving over the dunes in 4 wheel drive vehicles. The ability of some Saudi drivers to scale even the most difficult slopes is quite amazing.

The area is also home to a number of bedu who shepherd their sheep, goats and camels in the country surrounding the dunes.

Adding to the contrast in colours is the presence of a small number of irrigated farms growing feedstock. The vivid green of the fields contrasts beautifully with the red dunes and the tan/grey of the escarpment.

The "Red Sand Dunes" on the way to Hafirat Nisah, west of Riyadh.

This age old form of transport makes sense in the terrain around the Red Sands and more so when time is measured in other than hours and minutes.

A shepherd tends his flock on the Red Sands near Hafirat Nisah.

Opposite:
Frolicking in the sand is a favourite pastime, especially on a Friday holiday, for people of Riyadh.

Four wheel driving on the Red Sand Dunes near Hafirat Nisah.

Left and below right:
Spiny-tailed lizard (Uromastyx microlepis) called Dhab in arabic. It is considered by some bedu to be a delicacy and is hunted regularly. Its prehistoric head reminds one of a turtle's head.

Below left:
The home of the Dhab in the red sand dunes on the way to Hafirat Nisah.

66

One of the pretty aberrations around Riyadh is when you are travelling across a great distance of gravel hills and plains and come across a wide gully completely greened with trees, shrubs and reeds with a full flowing river in its midst. This is the result of the effluent of the Riyadh sewage treatment plant. The greened area covers a considerable distance and supports a large variety of bird and insect life. Many of the birds are resident there although the numbers are greatly increased during the migratory season with birds covering the route from Russia and Europe to Africa and vice versa. It is a wonderful early morning sight to see, virtually in the middle of the desert, large purple herons ranging up and down the river together with numbers of other species.

Purple heron (Ardea purpurea) at Al Hair river near Riyadh.

Left:
Female Moorhen
at Al Hair river.

Below:
Male Moorhen at
the same loca-
tion.

On a trip returning from Al Hair I ran across a young Saudi who was starting to train a very young peregrine falcon. The bird was quite restrained, tethered on his "post", and did not get too excited even when taunted by a live chicken.

In concluding this chapter on desert images of the Najd area it would not be complete without including some photos about, essentially, a desert celebration. Each year in March or early April a cultural festival and camel races are staged some 40 kilometres from Riyadh. The camel races are a particularly grand affair with several hundred camels starting in the main race and vying for a substantial first prize. The main race is staged over a distance of about 20 kilometres. The photos selected here are intended to give some idea of the pre-race build-up and the excitement of the race itself.

Opposite:
Camels out on a training walk prior to the race.
Below:
The crowd starts to gather early in the afternoon for the race which starts towards sundown.

Camels and riders on the way to the start of the camel race at the annual Al Janadriyah Cultural Festival near Riyadh.

Opposite left:
Little children having a picnic time watching all the activities leading up to the start of the camel race.

Opposite right:
A young hopeful rider mounted on his ride, waiting for instructions in the assembly yard.

Left:
Waiting time in the assembly yard prior to the starter's call.

Below right:
Under starter's orders - heading for the starting gates.

Below left:
Camel with Dust protection gear?

The starter attempts to get order before releasing the field.

The leading bunch thunders down the straight.

The leaders start on the last circuit of the 20 kilometre course.

Opposite:
The leading camels, after 17 kilometres, head for the final bend amidst the pall of dust thrown up by the camels and the hundreds of cars circling the track to keep up with their favourite. Although the sun has not yet gone down the riders are barely discernible.

National Guardsmen chase down their target mounts to hand their riders their placement baton.

CHAPTER THREE

NAFUD

The Great Nafud Desert occupies almost 20% of the Nafud Basin in the northeast of Saudi Arabia. Whilst this desert is only a small fraction of the size of the Rub al-Khali it has much of the same physical structure, i.e. longitudinal dunes known as uruq and high sand mountains. The sand in the Nafud is a reddish colour which stems from the high amount of iron oxide in the sand crystals.

Hail and Tabuk are the two largest communities which border onto the Nafud Basin while many small communities co-exist with the desert on its very edges.

When one is driving the route from Tabuk to Hail the countryside provides a geography and geology lesson. To begin with, on travelling southeast from Tabuk, one proceeds through many high dunes not far from Tabuk before entering a mountainous area where the hills are in various stages of being covered by sand blown up from further south.

The area from which the sand comes is a little like the "food supply" for the sand dunes. The area around Madain Saleh, for example, consists of sandstone mountains which have been eroding for centuries and providing more and more sand available to be blown with the prevailing winds. These winds mainly blow towards the Nafud and it is therefore not surprising that many hills are gradually being covered by sand.

I found myself asking the question, "How long would it take to cover one of these mountains with sand and, afterwards, how would you tell whether it was all sand or just a sand covered mountain". Perhaps a special survey would reveal the result but in the meantime it is very interesting to see the way nature is distributing its component parts, gradually changing the way the country looks. One thing is certain, there is certainly no shortage of sand for the Nafud with many billions of cubic metres of sand still to be eroded from the sand plains south of the Nafud.

Of particular interest to me was the extreme beauty of the dunes southeast of Tabuk. On the trip to Tabuk a sand storm raged and it was not possible to see the dunes. A few days later it was perfectly clear and the patterns and shapes of the dunes were exceptional.

There are a number of small villages out of Hail which are on the very edge of the Nafud. Jubbah is one of these and is interesting to see the bedu heading off into the Nafud itself where they live almost as they have done for centuries. Only the pickup truck and water tanker plus a few "town" luxuries make life a little easier.

There are many other small villages on the perimeter of the Nafud, all with the same problem - encroaching sand dunes. In some cases it is possible to see dwellings which have had to be abandoned because of the relentless flow of sand. It amazes me that the hardy folk there manage to eke out a living under such difficult circumstances. Many of the villages have their own charm, however, and one in particular had a lovely field with flowering blossom trees. It was a strange feeling to see such a sight on the very edge of the Nafud. But then, nature can show even the harshest environment in a good light sometimes.

The birth of a sand mountain on the way from Tabuk to Taima. These photos show the natural progression from rock mountain to sand mountain. Compare this with the sand mountains taken from the same general region (photos overleaf).

Opposite:
Tracks of bedu 4 wheel drives heading into the Nafud from the town of Jubbah, northwest of Hail.

Right:
A camel enclosed atop a large dune at the very edge of the Nafud near Jubbah.

A bedu 4 wheel drive pick-up truck heading for Jubbah from a desert camp.

An age-old style of camp with modern facilities near Hail.

A newly constructed mud brick building in Jubbah.

In Jubbah I noticed many new mud houses either constructed or being constructed. This was one of the few towns I have seen where the traditional building methods have survived on such a large scale. Certainly in the location on the edge of the Nafud the old houses have a much more environmentally friendly appearance than their modern counterparts.

Even the walls are constructed of mud and rocks. Perhaps the folks there have a very real understanding of their transient hold on the physical space called Jubbah.

Personally I like the look of a well constructed mud house more than a conventional western style house given the location in the proximity of the desert and date palms.

An old well in a fertile wadi in Jubbah.

Opposite:
The outskirts of the village of Umm Al Qulban on the edge of the Nafud - an uneasy balance between man and nature.

A camel vainly trying to fend off the flies in the heat of the day at Jubbah.

Springtime comes to the Nafud.

Flowering trees in the village of Umm Al Qulban west of Hail.

A dusty preview of the birth of another sand mountain on the road from Hail to Jubbah.

Abandoned houses in the shadow of an overwhelming body of Nafud sand close to Hail.

CHAPTER FOUR

RUB AL KHALI

The Rub al-Khali, or "Empty Quarter" as it is known, is reportedly the largest continuous stretch of sand desert in the world. It stretches from just west of Najran in the southern region of Saudi Arabia to UAE and Oman in the east. The western end is by far the most attractive with huge mountains of fine soft sand, often forming uruq (rows of sand mountains) interspersed by gravel plains with unusually large amounts of vegetation. In the east the desert altitude reduces significantly and dunes are interspersed with salt flats and flat sand plains.

Satellite photos show the uruq of the eastern end particularly well, especially just south of Wadi Ad Dawasir.

One of my most cherished memories of the Kingdom is a visit to the wildlife reserve of Uruq Bani Ma'arid which is south of Wadi Ad Dawasir atop the Jibal Tuwayq and right on the very edge of the Rub al-Khali. I would have previously thought this to be a most unlikely place to find a wildlife reserve but having seen it first hand I can understand why it is so ideal.

The reserve covers an area of about 12,000 square kilometres roughly in the shape of a hot air balloon. It is divided into three quite distinct zones. In a large segment on the western edge an area of 2,400 square kilometres is set aside as a strict nature reserve where grazing of animals, such as sheep, goats and camels, and hunting are strictly prohibited. A horseshoe shaped zone of 5,200 square kilometres allows controlled grazing while the eastern segment of 4,400 square kilometres is a hunting zone. The Reserve, under the control of the National Commission for Wildlife Conservation and Development is a novel experiment designed to secure a viable environment for previously endangered species, such as the Arabian Oryx, and, at the same time, provide a hunting area where bedu are permitted to pursue their centuries old hunting traditions.

Animals from the breeding programs operated by the Commission at Taif and Thumamah, near Riyadh, are released into the reserve. Among the animals released to date are the Oryx and Sand Gazelle. As well as the released animals the Reserve is home to a wide variety of other animals such as sand foxes, wolves, wild cats, hare, sand cats and, occasionally seen, the Hubara Bustard which is the focus of a significant breeding program at the Taif Wildlife Research Centre. The Jibal Tuwayq also holds a small population of Nubian Ibex although these are more likely to be seen at another of the Commission's Reserves at Howtat Bani Tamim.

Apparently an endemic species of ostrich was present in the past and the Taif centre is actively breeding ostriches as part of a long term goal to reintroduce them into the wild.

The first time impact of the Rub al-Khali with its huge sand mountains is breathtaking. The sheer size of the dunes when viewed from the plains in between the dunes is overpowering. The ability of the Saudi Rangers who patrol the reserve in 4 wheel drive vehicles is a marvel to behold. I can recall heading towards one sand mountain, similar to

Opposite:
Looking east inside the Wildlife reserve of Uruq Bani Ma'arid.

the second page of this Chapter, and thinking to myself "surely he isn't going up this mountain". But we did.

It was equally exciting to come over the top of a dune and stare down at the plain below before tearing headlong down the sand at what seemed to me to be about a 70 degree slope. I was told by my compatriot, however, that it would be more like 35 or 40 degrees. Either way, it was still impressive.

During the visit in the Reserve which extended about 40 kilometres into the Rub al-Khali we were fortunate enough to find a herd of Oryx and two herds of Sand Gazelles. The skill of the rangers in locating these animals was wonderful to behold. They also managed to find a sand fox, which had just emerged from its lair, and a falcon's nest in a tree.

Sand fox taking cover in the Uruq Bani Ma'arid Wildlife Reserve.

96

Arabian Oryx, part of a released herd, in the Wildlife Reserve of Uruq Bani Ma'arid.

Sand Gazelle in Uruq Bani Ma'arid reserve. The herd size seen was about 8-10 with several young animals in each herd.

Opposite:
The Tuwayq Escarpment near the entrance to the Wildlife Reserve of Uruq Bani Ma'arid.

Late afternoon shadows over the massive dunes of the Rub al-Khali.

After leaving Uruq Bani Ma'arid the road runs south before branching towards Najran in the southwest and Sharourah in the southeast. Taking the road towards Sharourah provides a memorable trip through about 250 kilometres of the Rub al-Khali with nothing but sand all around. But even there we found surprises. Whereas we would have expected to find egrets in the Reserve of Al Hair south of Riyadh where there is an abundance of water, we found four sitting on a road sign right in the middle of this long stretch of desert. They flitted backwards and forwards between two road signs as cars went past but seemed quite resigned, or contented, to remain there. Their only source of water could have been from a nearby bedu camp. The photo overleaf was the culmination of a comical series of movements where one bird was trying to prevent the other from keeping a foot hold on the road sign.

When the road reaches its southern extremity it turns west and runs along the uruq with huge dunes on either side of the road for many kilometres. The construction of this highway was a significant achievement given the harsh conditions existing there.

On the return trip we continued on towards Najran and encountered some beautifully patterned sand dunes.

99

Opposite:
The road to Sharourah through the Rub al-Khali.

Wind patterned sands between Sharourah and Najran in the Rub al-Khali.

Opposite:
Cattle Egrets battling for supremacy on top of a road sign in the Rub al-Khali.

As one approaches Najran the dunes of the Rub al-Khali gradually become smaller and give way to sand plains before encountering the mountains surrounding Najran. The picturesque town of Najran seems a world away from the Rub al-Khali. The very distinctive housing style of the area provides real character to the landscapes. On all the older style houses a terrace on the roof provides an ideal place to relax and enjoy the warm evening after sunset, drinking coffee and eating dates. Najran has an extremely old history dating back well over 2000 years. One can see many forts from a much later period dotting the mountain peaks as sentinels to the days when security on top of a mountain was as important in Najran as it was in other parts of the world. Winter time sees vast quantities of water flooding through parts of Najran and the fertility of the countryside is obvious with greenery and orchards everywhere.

The uruq of the Rub al-Khali gradually reducing in height as they approach the extremity of the desert towards Najran.

103

Opposite:
Facade of a multi story Najran building built in the traditional style.

Below:
Traditional style Najran houses showing the roof terraces. The green of the palms contrasts markedly with the stark black of the volcanic rock from an ancient era.

Above:
The outskirts of Najran showing the lush growth near the flood plain. Note the remnants of an old fort atop the mountain peak.

**Sandy plains lit-
tered with erod-
ing sandstone
outcrops, north-
east of Najran.**

On the road from Najran back to Sulayyil one passes through countryside very similar to that found in the vicinity of Madain Saleh. Large outcrops of eroding sandstone litter the sandy desert plains providing a seemingly inexhaustible supply of sand for the deserts. It is flat country, stretching kilometre after kilometre and even a mild wind whips waves of sand across the road before you.

After reaching the southern end of the Tuwayq Escarpment the road heads north again before reaching Wadi Ad Dawasir where it heads northeast towards Riyadh.

Shortly after this point we explored a wadi quite typical of any wadi located next to the escarpment and camped overnight. The location is really right on the edge of the Rub al-Khali but the two landscapes are very different.

**Fossil shell, mil-
lions of years old,
which has bro-
ken clear from its
"sarcophagus",
the escarpment.**

The eroding escarpment is made of sandstone and mudstone which, millions of years ago, was under water. This provides an interesting area to fossick looking for evidence of that bygone era. We found several samples of shells and coral fossils embedded in the mudstone, baked as hard as basalt by the blazing sun over the centuries.

Samples of fossil imprints from underwater vegetation or coral. This mudstone has been locked away inside the escarpment for millions of years and with erosion and decomposition over the centuries the imprints are revealed.

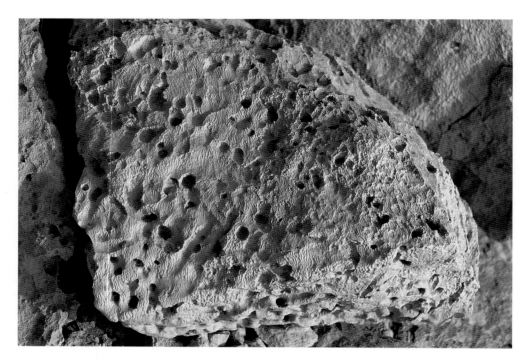

Opposite:
The view from the wadi near Sulayyil where the fossils were found. The Tuwayq Escarpment can be seen in the background.

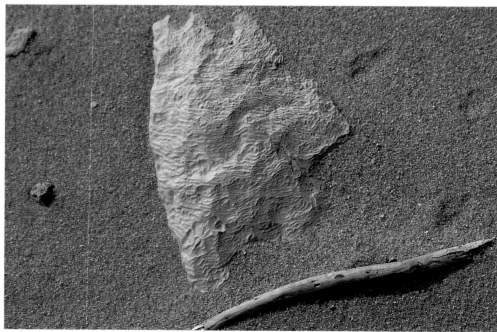

CHAPTER FIVE

HIJAZ

Previous page:
Looking towards
the Antiquities
area of Madain
Saleh.

The Hijaz is a region of great fascination for me. Not only because of its history but also because of the natural beauty of many places to be found there. I will always remember the sheer disbelief when I first set eyes on the landscapes around Madain Saleh and on subsequent trips I have found more and more unique landscapes to photograph.

As an example the photo on the second page of this Chapter was taken close to the Antiquities area of Madain Saleh. In fact Madain Saleh is actually just behind the hills in the background of the photo. A close examination of the photo will reveal sandstone, mudstone and volcanic rock of the strangest formation. The volcanic rock on the left hand side of the photo is a shell looking more like the nose cone of a rocket. The bands around the shell add to the fascination of the creation.

The mountains surrounding Madain Saleh, which has been my main area of fascination, have such wonderful shapes and in some ways remind one of the hills of Cappadocia in Turkey. Because of their unusual structures they provide an endless variety of possibilities when coupled with different lighting conditions.

I have noticed a big increase in the amount of farming around the Antiquities area in the last few years. While this adds its own charm it takes away from the wild and unspoilt look of a few years ago.

Without sandstorms the area can be

Sandstone out-
crops located
just outside the
Antiquities area
of Madain Saleh.

totally exhilarating to visit but if you are unfortunate to strike the wrong winds it can be a nightmare. I can remember spending one day and night in the area when the sun or stars were hardly visible through the howling sand. The following morning the winds had died down and the day was perfect.

The early morning colours around Madain Saleh can be quite subtle and fleeting. The photo below was taken about 20 minutes after sunrise and the result is a landscape similar to that which would have been painted by the famous aboriginal painter from Australia, Albert Namatjira. After a further 20 minutes, however, the same photo was washed out and lifeless. I am sure that one could continue to find different photographic subjects and conditions on successive trips to the area.

As usual, the local Saudi people are very friendly. I was just about to set up a tent on one occasion and a farmer stopped and told me it would be better for me to stay at his house. I greatly enjoyed his hospitality and spent a magical night on a comfortable bed under the stars.

Looking away from near the main entrance of the Antiquities area of Madain Saleh.

Opposite:
Sunrise over
Madain Saleh.

A buildup of dust
around Madain
Saleh heralded
the imminent
arrival of a howl-
ing storm which
raged most of
the night.

Opposite:
A green farm emerges from what was previously sandy desert surrounding Madain Saleh.

A new camp nestles under the lee of the huge mudstone mountains surrounding Madain Saleh.

This acacia tree seems to hold a particular attraction for this herd of camels near Al Ula, just south of Madain Saleh.

Opposite:
Some of the sandstone massifs which rise vertically from the sandy plains of Madain Saleh.

The buildings of the Madain Saleh Railway Station restored by the Department of Antiquities. Behind stand the ever-present massive sandstone mountains.

Opposite: These eroded plateau are just before Al Ula, south of Madain Saleh. The photo was taken as the sand was beginning to swirl as a prelude to a full-blooded sandstorm.

Mudstone cliffs near Madain Saleh gradually eroding away. In the foreground are rocks of volcanic origin.

Above:
White camels
grazing near
Madain Saleh.

Left:
A camel rider
rounds up his
herd of camels
for the return to
camp overnight.

Near Madain Saleh. The early morning sun catches sandstone sentinels rising from the plain as far as the eye can see.

Opposite:
One of the most striking tombs in Madain Saleh. It stands apart from the majority of the tombs and is the only tomb carved in this solitary sandstone massif.

Left:
Near the Diwan in Madain Saleh.

Left:
A sandstone massif rises vertically from the plain near Madain Saleh.

Below:
An unusual rounded facade and another "normal" facade under construction.
Stonemasons worked from the top down in order to have a working platform.

Madain Saleh (cities of Saleh) itself is in the Al-Hijr Valley. The Nabataean civilisation which built the remnants we see today is the same ancient Arab tribe which built Petra in Jordan. The age of the settlement is about 2000 years and was built after Petra which was the capital of the Nabataean Kingdom when it was at its peak. Its fortune resulted from the strategic location of Petra on the trade route from Yemen. No less strategic was Madain Saleh. The skill of the stone masons is obvious and whilst the creations in Petra are more sophisticated the tombs here are still impressive.

The settings the Nabataeans chose for their cities was exceptional. There are many similarities between Petra and Madain Saleh in that they are both in areas where impressive and often solitary sandstone mountains rise out of the plain providing the very building blocks needed for the carving of the Nabataeans. The magnificent tombs seen in Madain Saleh are the result.

Opposite:
Tombs carved in the sandstone of Al-Hijr at Madain Saleh.

The Diwan, or Meeting Place, is a huge room carved into the sandstone. Seats are arranged around the walls. The narrow pass in the rocks (so reminiscent of the Siq at Petra) leads to the "High places" where sacrifices of animals took place, as at Petra.

Right:
Carved tomb
facades showing
different styles of
entrance and
also different lev-
els of affluence
of the owners.

Below:
Niches carved in
the tomb walls to
receive the
coffins of family
members of the
owner of the
tomb.

As one heads south from Madain Saleh the landscape changes dramatically from the huge sandstone mountains of Al-Hijr. The photo below was taken 40 kms south of Al-Hijr while the one on page 129 was taken about 80 kms south. The gravel plains are in stark contrast with the sand and sandstone of Al-Hijr.

Left:
Desert landscape about 40 kilometres south of Madain Saleh.

Opposite:
Desert landscape about 80 kilometres south of Madain Saleh.

Opposite:
It is images such as these taken south of Madain Saleh that have captivated me over a long period of time. I saw them originally on a trip when lighting conditions were not right and I vowed to return. Fortunately on the next trip the conditions were much better.

Above and right:
The total solitude of these plains about 80 kilometres south of Madain Saleh has to be experienced to fully understand the timeless nature of the region.

This landscape is similar to that which the Hijaz Railway traverses on its way to Madinah. The successive layers of mountains as they climb towards the west is a wonderful sight at sunset.

Further south of Madain Saleh the route of the Main Road to Madinah runs parallel, for some little distance, to the route of the old Hijaz Railway which operated between Damascus in Syria and Madinah from 1908 until 1917 when it came under increasing attack from combined British and Arab forces.

Turkish forces who held Madinah at the time of the 1st World War used the railway to resupply their garrison there and at the many minor stations along the route.

During its life the trains of the Hijaz carried many hundreds of thousands of Pilgrims to Madinah under conditions much less arduous than the previous camel trains which were used to undertake the journey. The railway was not without its risks, however, and trains were subjected initially to spasmodic raids from tribesmen.

As the war continued it became a target of the British and Arab forces with the British strategist T.E. Lawrence playing a major role. His idea was to cause just enough damage through mining the line to enable the Turks to keep the line open but with great difficulty.

This strategy succeeded with continual attacks progressing towards Damascus as the war proceeded and finally the Turks gave up using the line.

It is fascinating to follow the line of the railway from a point some 80 kilometres south of Madain Saleh to a point some 50 kilometres north of Madinah. The line itself has now disappeared as have the steel sleepers but there are several trains in various states of repair along the length of the line and the string of extremely well built stations together

Above:
The main railway station at Madain Saleh which is being progressively restored by the Department of Antiquities to excellent condition. The line from Damascus to Madain Saleh was opened in 1907 followed by Madinah in 1908.

Left:
One of the stations on the Hijaz railway, which were spaced about every 18 kms. along the route.
South of Al Ula for some distance, the stations were constructed of sandstone which was readily available from Madain Saleh. Further south the material changes to almost black basalt.

with the bridges and culverts make interesting exploration.

The quality of workmanship of the railway construction workforce under the direction of German Engineer Messner was excellent as the photos show. Even the culverts spaced along the track, and which would not have been visible to the train passengers, are of the highest quality. Most of them are still standing today after seventy five years of no maintenance.

Opposite:
This train, blown up by British and Arab troops, is just south of Mashad station. Because of the dry desert air, it is still in an excellent state of preservation.

Above and left:
These fine examples of masonry culvert construction can be seen on the Hijaz Railway south of Al Ula.

Opposite:
These photos show the extent of damage to this mined train south of Mashad station. It is probable that it was exploded by a raiding party under the command of Garland of the British Army since he had succeeded with his first automatic mine under a troop train just south of this location at Toweira station.

One of the stations further from the sandstone of Madain Saleh. The black basalt makes an imposing and sombre building. The quality of workmanship was still maintained at a very high level even though the working of the basalt would have been much more difficult than the sandstone.

These "ballast" storage heaps are still as perfect as when they were laid out 75 years ago. The stones were used to top up the railway bed along the length of the track and were strategically placed at several places along the route.

The convoy is lined up before a substantial sand drift about 400 metres long and 20 metres high across the route of the railway line

<u>Opposite:</u>
Bridge & ruins of a Turkish Fort just before the Hadiyah Station.

All that was required was a little confidence, good speed and, to be absolutely sure, a little less air in the tyres. No-one had any difficulty in crossing.

In the photo below the train was, until only a few years ago, upright on the spur line at Hadiyah Station. The station is located in a very picturesque wadi covering many square kilometres. A steel sleeper can be seen in front of the train. Most of these from the entire railroad have been used by bedu for various building purposes.

In the photo on the right the spur line can be seen joining the main line which runs in front of the station on towards Madinah. The dunes, just visible in the background, stretch from the hill behind the station and a climb up to the top late in the afternoon revealed a most wonderful sight. The photo on page 141 was the result. It appears more like a lunar landscape but it captures the rugged beauty of the mountains of the Hijaz as well as the softness of the dunes dotted about along the route.

Left:
Spur line at Hadiyah station.

Opposite:
Looking westwards in the late afternoon over the dunes near Hadiyah station.

Right:
Train lying on its side on the spur line at Hadiyah station. Behind the tender can be seen a railway car with timber laterals still in place. This is most unusual along the Hijaz railway. Perhaps the only other place where this might be seen is at the station in Madinah.

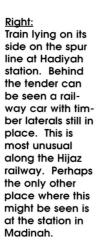

Right:
Complete train standing on tracks in front of Buwayr station north of Madinah.

Below:
Looking towards the locomotive from a box car of the train at Buwayr.

Below:
Architectural detail of a stairway in one of the stations built from black basalt stone. The quality of workmanship is obvious.

Khaybar Dam, about 20kms south of the town of Khaybar. This large ancient dam is still complete except for the breach shown here. The other side of the dam can be seen on the right side of the bottom photo. These gullies transfer a tremendous amount of run-off water in the rainy season.

A strange layered effect on rocks in one of the pools near the Khaybar Dam.

Near Khaybar the volcanic past of the region is in evidence. Lava fields such as those seen in this photo stretch to the horizon.

Even more dramatic than the above photo is this farm established in a wadi between Jeddah and Madinah in the midst of mountains and an extensive lava field from an ancient volcano.

A major station on the Hijaz railway was at Tabuk. The station itself has been retained partly as a restored park. The region around Tabuk, however, has some very attractive desert scenery with huge mountains as one heads to Duba on the coast. On one trip we found a fascinating piece of desert just off the main road with interesting rock formations and sandstone patterns. Earlier in the same day the dust was so bad that the dawn revealed a day that was more like an eclipse and produced an eerie series of photos.

A dust storm covers the early morning sun between Tabuk and Duba.

A sandstone out-
crop between
Tabuk and Duba
on a dusty day.
The extensive
outcrop yielded
a wide variety of
different sand-
stone patterns
and colours.

"Pinnochio" with his hat and long nose carved out of a sandstone outcrop in the desert close to Tabuk.

CHAPTER SIX

THE DESERT IN MINIATURE

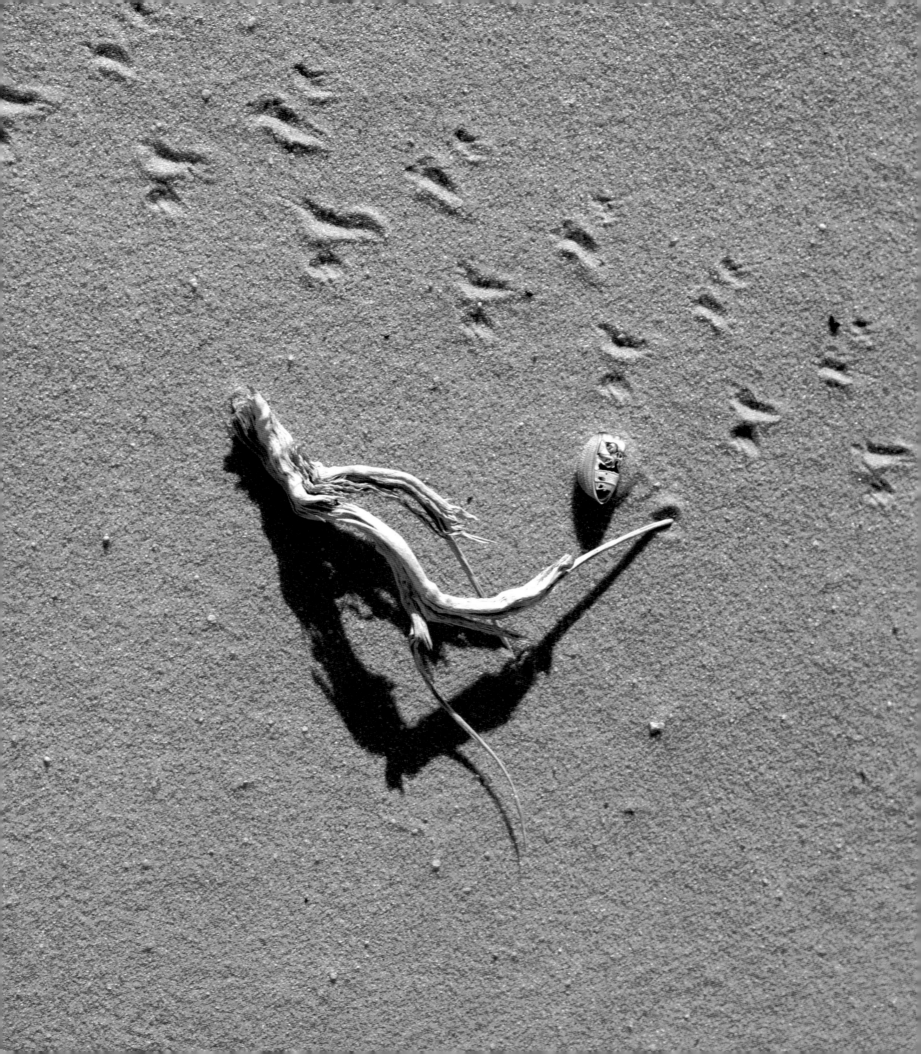

There are some extremely interesting miniature photographic opportunities to be found in the desert. Some are simply dramatic abstract compositions while others have a more historical connection. Either way the photos represent views that can only be seen by taking time and viewing the desert and its surroundings with great care and dedication. It seems quite surprising, for example, to find such a healthy plant shooting out of the sand as in the photo below, and yet, after good seasonal rains, the sand dunes burst into life with a wide range of plant life. Wherever there is plant life one will find abundant insect life as well. They can create their own magical images as in the ant nests opposite. Animal tracks also present some wonderful sand abstracts.

Left:
New succulent growth emerges from rain watered sand near Dilim, south of Riyadh.

Right:
Desert locust (Schistocera gregaria).

Opposite top left:
These ants' nests would appear to the ants like two volcanoes rising out of the sand.

Opposite Top Right:
A commonly found beetle (Adesmia sp.) in Rawdhat Kareem.

Right:
Sand tracks in dunes near Dilim.

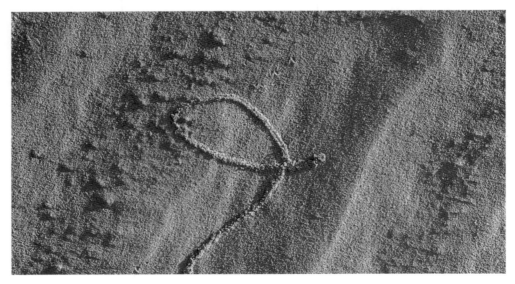

Opposite bottom left:
The delicate white flowers of Cleome amblyocarpa in a desert area south of Ar Rass.

Opposite bottom right:
Eagle tracks in the sand south of Madain Saleh. Dunes are a common hunting ground for eagles throughout the Kingdom. Note the difference in sand colour from that at Ad Dahna.

The head of this thistle (Echinops spinosa) ultimately becomes a spikey ball which can often be seen rolling in the wind across the desert floor.

Colourful beetles photographed south of Ar Rass in the Qassim region.

Croscherichia salavatiani

Mylabris (Euzonabris) maculiventris

Right:
Launaea angusti-
folia

Below left:
Teucrium oliveri-
anum

Below right:
Matthiola sp.

Above:
Painted Lady butterfly "Vanessa cardui" on the dunes of Ad Dahna.

Left:
A 'metallic' coloured beetle on an acacia tree in a wadi near Sulayyil, southwest of Riyadh.

This "Bonsai" tree
was found in a
wadi near
Sulayyil south-
west of Riyadh.

If you look closely at this photo you will see the end of the tail of a Lacertid (Acanthodactylus schmidti). It had burrowed into the seemingly firm ground in an instance when I approached beyond its comfort level.

Centipede entering a hole after being disturbed near an escarpment outside of Riyadh.

<u>Opposite:</u>
A gerbil found with a flash light during a night search in dunes near Dilim. It did not seem to mind the light and continued to feed on grass seeds and scurried in and out of its hole. The bright flash of the camera made it jump for a second and it then continued its business.

<u>Below:</u>
This almost transparent spider was found in the Ad Dahna dunes east of Riyadh.

<u>Left:</u>
A beetle (Pycnodactylus tomentosus) in the dunes at Ad Dahna.

<u>Below:</u>
The dung beetle is seen in cooler months, as here, rolling balls of dung for its young larvae to feed on. It walks backwards, rolling the ball with its hind legs.

159

One of the strangest desert miniatures to be found in Saudi Arabia exists about 30 kilometres beyond Khurais towards Hofuf. A short distance from the road can be found remains of sharks and other marine life which existed there some 40 - 55 million years ago in the Eocene age. At that time the area was an underwater reef and, although the fossils require careful searching and some luck to find good specimens, it would be unusual not to find at least some during a visit. There are several different types of sharks teeth to be found as indicated on the opposite page.

One of the other finds which I found just as fascinating was shells which were composed of volcanic rock. I believe the process for forming these was that shells became trapped in sand which formed a cast similar to that used for casting molten metals today. As underwater lava found its way through the sand it entered the cast and ate away the calcium of the shell leaving a replica lava shell which then cooled in the cast. They can be found in all shapes and sizes and the whole area makes for a most exciting treasure hunt during the cooler autumn and spring months.

Below:
View of the ancient reef area east of Khurais where the sharks teeth and "lava" shells can be found.

Opposite :
The left photo is a Porbeagle shark's tooth from the ancient reef area while the right photo is of Sand shark's tooth.

Opposite:
Sample "lava" shells recovered from the ancient reef area near Khurais.

Opposite page:
Top left -
Cross-section of
Echinops sp.

Top right -
Malva sp.

Bottom left -
Calotropis pro-
cera

Bottom right -
Rumex vesicarius

Top Left:
Zilla spinosa
showing new
growth.

Top right:
Nymph
grasshopper.

Right:
Mushrooms near
Dawadmi.

CHAPTER SEVEN

THE ARTISTRY OF NATURE

This chapter is dedicated to the artistry of nature, particularly in relation to sand, sandstone and mud where the most wonderful abstract creations can be found. Some are fleeting as they are composed from the light of a short segment of time, usually in the early morning. Others are the result of ages of erosion while yet others are created from short term happenings such as floods. This is but a small sample of what nature has to offer.

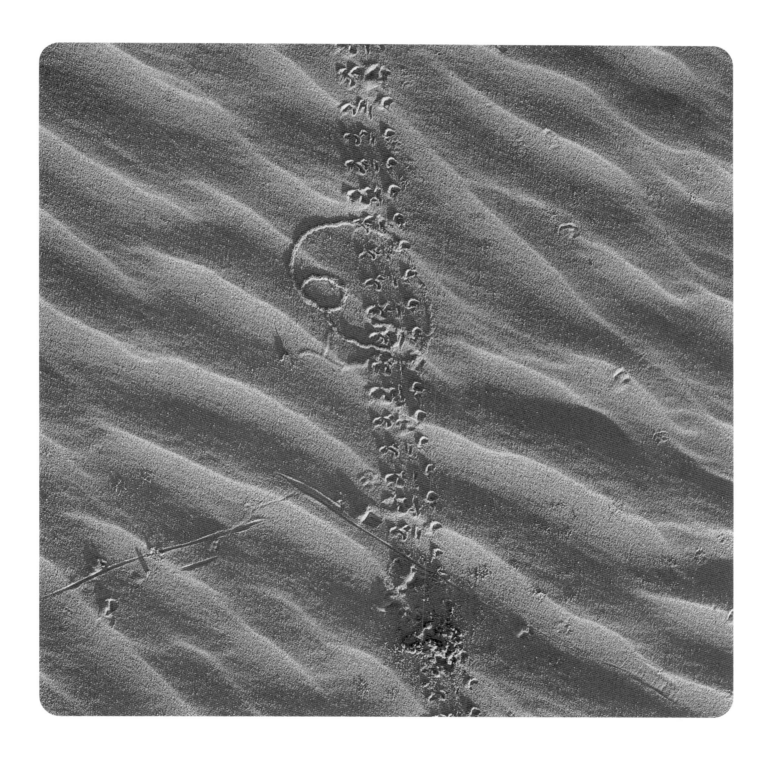

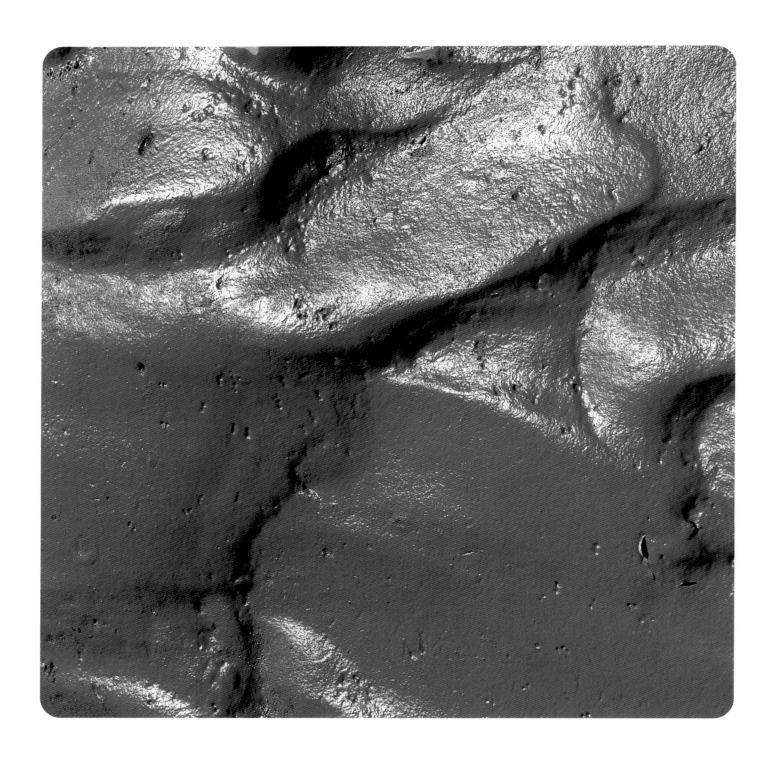

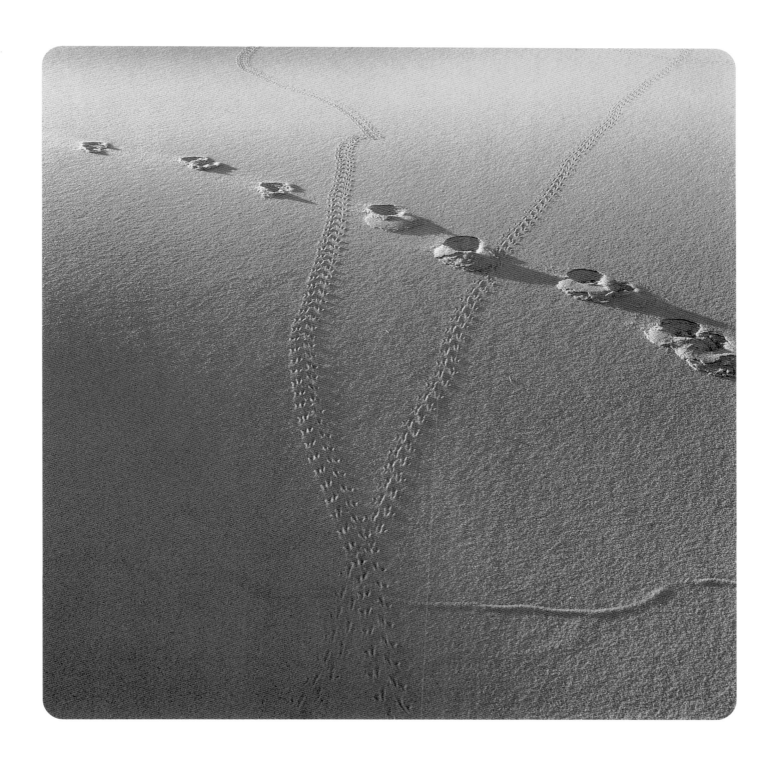

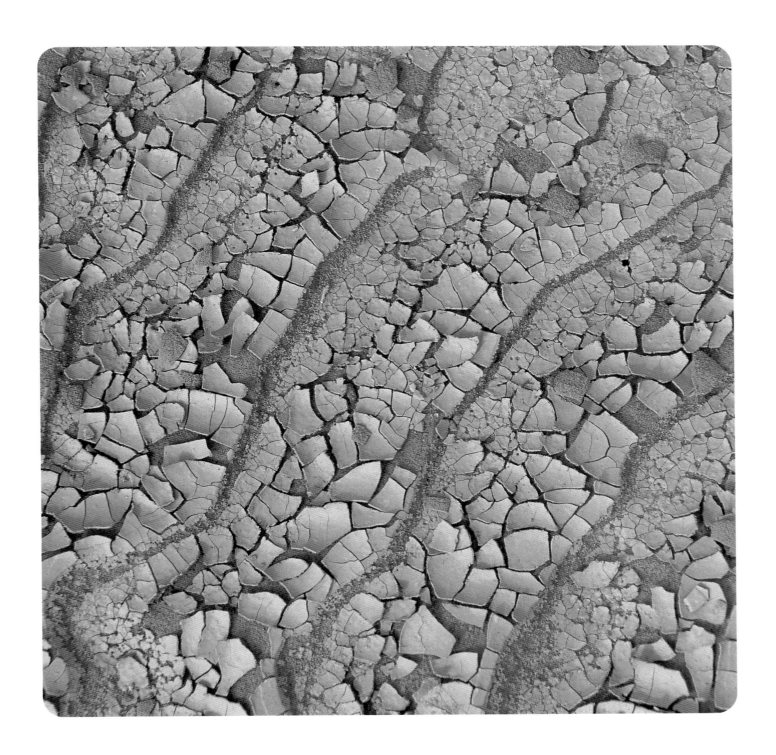

I would like to express my sincere appreciation to the following people
for their assistance during the preparation of this book.

Professor Dr. Abdulaziz Hamed Abu Zinada for his interest in my work and his encouragement about photographing wild life in the Kingdom. I wish to also thank his many staff who have assisted in one way or another. The staff of Uruq Bani Ma'arid, particularly Al Homaij Ali Al-Sayari and Mohamad Al-Baroudi, for their assistance and friendship in showing us with great pride their domain in the Empty Quarter. Also from the NCWCD, Dr. Tarik Al-Abassi, Dr. Qutaiba Al-Sadoon and Dr. H.S.A. Yahya for their identification of flora and birds in the book.

The Directorate General of the Agriculture and Water Resources Research Centre in Riyadh, particularly Dr. Shaukat Ali Chaudhary for his assistance in identifying some of the insects included in the book, and also Fahad Al-Ebdin for his help.

Mohammed Babelli for his friendship, advice and indispensible help with many facilitation matters without which the publication of this book would have been a much more difficult task.

Stein Tumert for his permission to use the jacket photo of the Author taken near Dukhneh, for his companionship during many productive photographic expeditions in many parts of the Kingdom and for his invaluable help in setting up the computer arrangement for doing the page layouts for the book.

Assem Al Sabban for his ongoing encouragement in improving my photography and for his ever-ready advice and assistance over a long period of time.

George Kawand for his help in many ways, especially his assistance with the transportation of the computer equipment I used for the page layouts for the book and his tireless help in chasing things for me in the USA.

A number of people including Mohamed Al-Dahlaan, Ameer Al-Jibreen, Naif Al-Qahtani, Mohammad Al-Taum and Muratib for their assistance in various ways.

Lastly, but by no means least, my wife Annelies for her patient support both during photographic expeditions, when she performed the roles of critic, carrier and expert spotter, and at home during the many hours spent on photographic work and with the computer doing page layouts and mockups. She also very capably performed the exacting and tedious task of press-check with the Printer.

Bibliography

1. Mitchell Beazley in association with the IUCN - The World Conservation Union. *Deserts, The Encroaching Wilderness. 1993*

2. Mark Shephard. *The Simpson Desert.* Reed Books, Sydney, 1992.

3. Betty A. Lipscombe Vincett. *Animal life in Saudi Arabia, 1982.*

4. Royal Commission for Jubail and Yanbu. *Wild Plants of Jubail and Yanbu.*

5. Marycke Jongbloed. *The Living Desert.* Motivate Publishing, Dubai, 1987.

6. Christian Gross. *Mammals of the Southern Gulf.* Motivate Publishing, Dubai, 1987.

7. T.E. Lawrence. *Seven Pillars of Wisdom.* Penguin.

8. Robert Graves. *Lawrence and the Arabs.* Paragon House, New York.

9. Royal Commission for Jubail and Yanbu. *Birds of Madinat Yanbu Al-Sinaiyah and its hinterland.*

10. National Guard King Khalid Hospital Bushwackers and Landtrekkers League notes on Madain Saleh and the Hijaz Railway.

11. Tcheko Minosa, Patricia Massari and Cherbel Dagher. *Najran, Desert Garden of Arabia.* Scorpio Editeur.

12. Ionis Thompson. *Desert Treks from Riyadh.* Stacey International, London, 1994.